the tale of walter
the pencil man

the tale of walter the pencil man

Ian McMillan
and Tony Husband

STACK
BOOKS

Smokestack Books
PO Box 408, Middlesbrough TS5 6WA
e-mail: info@smokestack-books.co.uk
www.smokestack-books.co.uk

The Tale of Walter the Pencil Man
Text copyright 2013, Ian McMillan
Cartoons copyright 2013, Tony Husband.
All rights reserved.

Author photograph by Adrian Mealing

Printed and bound by Martins the Printers Ltd,
Berwick-upon-Tweed.

ISBN 978-0-9575747-1-7

Middlesbrough
moving forward

Smokestack Books is represented by Inpress Ltd

*This book is dedicated to Joseph Fletcher
who died on the Somme on 1 July 1916.
He was twenty-four.*

Imagine this: A pit village, 1914;
A row of houses standing in the cold.
A covering of snow has settled on the green
A winter sun is shining like fool's gold.
Men are standing, talking, in the Queen's Head yard;
The air is tight and frosty and the sky is hard.

Picture this: a sea of sludge, 1917;
You just can't see the army for the dirt.
Stumbling through the morning like a war machine
Built from fear and trembling, blood and hurt.
Look closely though; familiar faces loom through fog.
Silence snapped in two by a barking dog.

Something links these worlds across the seasons, the years;
A long unbroken line from there to there
Those Queen's Head boys with nervous laughter, foaming beers
Grins like horses, windswept ruffled hair;
And those stumbling zombies with faces like screams
That populate your night times, infiltrate your dreams.

Look closer; see that soldier with the nervous eyes
That pit lad with the pencil in his hand
Time and pain buzzed round them like a swarm of flies
They marched down to the station with the band
And the snow fell down like feathers, freezing white
Then the train rolled through the farmland in the night

And if this was a film the screen would shake and shift;
We'd have a montage of different scenes
Some marching, some shouting, a time of endless drift
Peeling potatoes, digging the latrines:
But always we see Walter drawing as he peels,
Drawing as he polishes and right-wheels.

An officer's looking at the troops in the rain
A kindly sergeant points him Walter's way,
Says 'this lad's an artist, with an artist's brain
His drawings seem to have something to say.'
And the Captain glares at Walter and shouts 'Boy,
A pencil's not a weapon; a gun's not a toy.'

Walter nods, salutes. The officer stares him down
Then turns and quickly marches through the camp;
His nose is elongated and his eyebrows frown
Above two eyes that flicker like a lamp
Outside a brothel. Well, that's what Walter sees
When he draws the brass hat later, pad on his knees.

All his mates gather round and laugh like drunken fools
As he spreads his cartoons across the bed;
They didn't teach this kind of art at miner's schools
No art at all in fact. Just fear and dread
And the knowledge that a life spent down the pit
Would see you drop down in a cage to shovel shit.

But how many of these lads could have been poets,
Musicians, artists, chefs or merely those
Who appreciate an artwork and who know it
Makes life glow brightly in its brighter clothes?
We'll never know. The coal mine drew them tighter
And the war transformed these face men into fighters

Except our Walter; fighting's not his game. He draws
As other people breathe and drink and eat
To soften the sharp teeth of war, fighting's awful claws
That rip apart the town square and the street.
His papers fill with Colonels looking daft.
The sergeant got a clip because he laughed.

An officer arrives one drizzly morning
To inspect a ragged line of freezing blokes,
Belching, farting, scratching, swearing, yawning;
The officer begins to crack a joke
About the Germans being scared of bully beef
Because eating babies had destroyed their teeth

And no one laughs. The faces stay the same:
Turned inward, frowning, wishing they were gone
To somewhere far from this war's awful game
To somewhere peaceful, somewhere in the sun.
Then the officer knocks something from his coat
And looks ahead, and clears his coddled throat

And tells the men the news they didn't want:
'Tomorrow, lads, you'll all be marching out
To take your places right along the front
God save the King: now let me hear you shout
God save the King!' The line mumbles in a voice
That speaks of years of silence, lack of choice.

The officer grows angry, and his face
Gets redder than a sunset by a fire.
He bellows out 'You men are a disgrace!'
He squeaks. He pipes. His voice is rising higher
Until it seems to break and, like a sheet
Of glass it shatters by his polished feet.

The silence hangs like smoke after a bomb.
The silence drifting like a freezing fog
Covers up the officer: he's gone
His tail between his khaki like a dog.
That's how Walter draws him later, as the night
Frames the distant gunfire's breaking light.

The front: that hell of blood and noise and mud
And shattered skulls gaping in cries and screams
And eyes that say 'We never understood
Why we were here. Is this some stinking dream
From which we'll wake and find we're here again
As horror and regret fall down like rain?'

The front. A map-drawn line that must be crossed
At dawn by stumbling lions led by mules
Who watch and scream as some kid's body's tossed
Into exploding air then lands in pools
Of blood and sludge and filthy thoughtless water.
War's just a word. Another word is slaughter.

Thin sleep that night. A full moon lights the faces
Of those who lie and stare at God knows what.
They look inward. They're journeying to places
Defined by roaring shells, a single shot
That takes them through the brain or through the heart.
A bugle sounds. The day's about to start.

Walter wakes and packs his pencil and some paper;
Hides them somewhere in the bottom of his pack
So that one morning he might stop and shape a
Drawing in the pause between attacks.
A simple shape or two, a joke, a funny word
That takes this waste and makes it seem absurd.

They march. Above, a bird wheels in the sky
And throws a song unheeding to the air
And men below march down the road to die:
The song fades out in patterns of despair.
And not too far away the guns' dull dreadful sound
Shakes the air and rumbles in the ground.

The trench: a slit dug in a field of sludge.
The trench: a landscape of boredom and of fear.
The trench: a stride becomes a trudge.
The trench: a jaded eye, a listening ear.
The trench: a world within a world within a world.
The trench: a tattered flag ignored as it's unfurled.

In a quiet moment halfway through a day
That's veered from 'Stand ready!' to 'Men, stand down!'
Walter draws and finds something to say
In an image of an officer in town
Ordering a drink at a bombed-out bar
Saying 'I think the troops are safer where they are.'

The night's the worst. The night before the sun
Pokes above the trenches like a flare,
The night before the shouting, the night before the run
That might just help your dash from here to there
Or might just send you screaming to a place
That leaves you with an absence where you used to have a face.

The night's so quiet. Quiet as a book-filled room
That invites you to come in, come in and read.
This is the quiet that sleeps just before the doom
Just before the sunrise makes the nightscape bleed.
Walter sits in silence, and Walter's beating heart
Wants the battle to be over. But the fight's about to start.

Walter thinks back to the pit, the day the cage-wire failed
And fifteen of his workmates shot down to their deaths:
It seemed the earth's core shuddered, paused, and then inhaled
All those lives and all those dreams in gasping, heaving breaths
And the silence that followed was like this silent night
Waiting in the night-cage, falling to first light.

And Walter did what Walter did: he began to draw
A pithead and some miners waiting to go down
But it wasn't coal they dug; these pitmen mined for WAR
And pumped out blood to make their workmates drown.
Walter looks at the page then tears it into pieces
And in the eastern sky, the quarter-light increases.

And somewhere just across the mud, in another hole
Another hand is making marks on a scrap of wood.
Another talent brought down to the fingers from the soul
Another way to shape the world, to make it understood.
Lars, a boy from Germany whose talent and whose skill
Was more for drawing than saluting or pack drill.

He had some paper but he lost it when they had to move
Down the line or up the line; it fluttered, disappeared
So now he draws on wood because his officers approve
Of what he does. 'It gives the men good cheer'
A General said, his awkward, formal speech
Trying to hold his screams in as above the bullets screeched.

If we looked at the trenches now, we'd simply be amazed
How close they were, how tiny was the gap
Between them both in morning's early hanging haze
Half-an-inch apart on hand drawn maps
That Generals pointed to with studied ease:
'We'll go from here. Beyond those stunted trees…'

Suddenly the morning's broken, sunlight fills the sky
A sergeant puts a whistle to his lips
And Walter and his shaking mates stand up to run and die
And panic grabs their balls and squeezes, grips
And leaves them hauling air into their rasping lungs.
There's a ladder up the trench. Death has carved the rungs.

Lars is frightened, too. He sees the running men
Coming through the smoke; he feels so sick.
His mouth is drier than a desert. He swallows, spits again
His lips are cracked, he wets them with a lick
Then lifts his rifle and takes careful aim
At a stumbling figure. This is not a game.

Walter runs but can't see where he's going.
He could be moving sideways, turning back,
The noise is building slowly; growing, growing
As this tense morning boils into attack
And the flower of England and Germany's youth
Face the butcher's cleaver of the bleeding truth.

Lars gets Walter in his sights. Pauses. Wipes his eyes
And in that fractured instant Walter's gone
Into the smoke and shouting, the heart-destroying cries
As Walter's friends are smashed down one by one
Like skittles in the alley at the Old Queen's Head
Where Walter and his mates would say 'Lots more Jerry dead!'

Before they turned to Nancy and she pulled another drink.
Walter caught her eye and she seemed to smile;
Then he tipped his miner's cap and offered her a wink
As innocent as morning, free from worldly guile.
A wink, that's all, to a girl he'd known from school
When he called her a witch and she called him a fool.

And when they marched away that morning down the street
There she was amongst the cheering crowd
Waving and shouting above the pounding feet
And she caught Walter's eye and mouthed 'I'm proud'
And his heart swelled fit to bust; he raised his hat
The crowd swept on. He thought that might be that.

But early in his time across the sea in France
He got a letter from her, full of village news:
The parson and a lady at the Friday dance
The pit's new wheel, the farmer's good prize ewes
And Walter told himself that he would send her art:
His cartoons. But he never did. And it broke his heart.

Reality explodes and shatters Walter back to war
Back from Nancy and her gorgeous smile
To this present hell: this rumbling, this roar.
This wide carpet of bodies spread right across the mile
Today's supposed to conquer. Lanky Tom is dead.
There's a space in the morning that used to be his head.

Walter falls into a hole and suddenly the sound
Changes; seems to come from far away
Beyond this shallow foxhole scooped out of the ground,
Beyond this blood-bathed morning, and the day
That began with a single bird flying through the air
And will end in moaning and blank despair.

Lars can shoot no more; hands are shaking like the wings
Of a butterfly that sets down on a leaf.
His ears are blank with deafness and his right eye stings.
He's aching and he's praying for relief
From the noise and the pain of this terrible hour
That's endless in its thoughtless power.

In his hole Walter's clambering to the slippery brink
As something in his head begins to hurt;
He thinks back to the Queen's Head. He'd really love a drink
And there's something crawling down his filthy shirt.
He pulls out his paper and then begins to draw
To capture something just this side of shock and awe.

This could have been a strange sight, I think you'll agree;
Above, the air is thick with bombs and smoke
And in the filthy foxhole with his paper on his knee
Walter's drawing something: not a joke,
Not a line to make you laugh; more a comment or a thought
That must be put on paper, must be rounded up and caught

Before it blows away in the yelling and the breeze
Before the moment's shot down like a frightened lad.
Walter draws a soldier standing by the trees
Who could be anybody's husband, anybody's Dad
And he's holding up a feather to the burning sky
Because he doesn't want to be here, he doesn't want to die.

Lars sees Walter drawing from the confines of his trench;
Walter chews his pencil; Lars recognises this
As a common human gesture rising high above the stench
And the grip of the battles all-embracing kiss.
Tears stream down his face, mingle with the spit
That's dribbling down his chin and dropping in the shit.

Lars does something scary. Something foolish. Something mad.
He clambers from the trench, runs across the dirt
To where Walter is drawing a small image of his dad
Trying to cover Walter from the pain and hurt
That war is pouring down onto his son's pale head
Lars says nothing but begins to draw instead.

Impossible, I suppose, far-fetched. A fantasy
A made up 'Angels of Mons' type tale
That's nothing more than a fictional story
You can tell the kids when you've had some ale.
But Walter and Lars sat and drew that day
And they didn't speak. And they had plenty to say.

Somehow what they drew came from both their hearts.
Somehow what they drew was louder than a gun.
One would finish something that the other seemed to start,
They knew what they were doing though they'd only just begun.
Walter drew. Lars drew. They drew together:
Something happened there that day. A change in the weather.

A pause occurred; not silence, or near silence, but a shift
In the noise that shook the ground and broke the sky.
And in a moment Lars was gone like smoke goes from a drift
To a breath of nothing, fading like a memory of a sigh.
He dropped his pencil as he ran. It lay there. Walter turned
And picked it up and kept it as the dark air throbbed and burned.

This is a moment, in a harsh and pointless war
When something changes, when art is moved along
And taken to a place it hasn't been before
Like when walking turned to dance, a shout became a song;
Like when the poets of world War One
Held the future in their verses because the past had gone.

We all know the story: how the young poets changed;
How Owen and Brooke had their lives turned round
How in the face of war the very language rearranged
And poetry was fashioned that recognised the sound
Of bullets and bombs and weeping and worse
Could be fashioned and bullied and shaped into verse.

Walter was drawing till the page almost caught fire:
One of a solider holding out a helping hand
As the pile of bodies round him grew bloodily higher.
One of a copse of severed limbs growing from the land.
Something altered in Walter that morning; something came
Close to Walter's ringing ear and whispered Walter's name.

Maybe that's what happens in the blast and sweat of war,
Your mind pulls up new ideas from somewhere deep inside.
Something can be thought of that's not been thought before
Other pathways can be walked on, other methods tried.
Or is this just a young kid doing the only thing he can
Drawing might be the answer when you haven't got a plan.

Time passes. Someone shouts 'Cease fire!' Silence broods
Across the field of battle, then the shouting starts
As quietness falls clean away, reality intrudes
Into the scene. Life expires from piles of broken hearts.
And Walter's found alive and dazed, pencil in his hand
A look scratched on his face that says he cannot understand

How people could do this to other people, how this war
Has pushed us the brink of what our bodies can withstand
Has forced us in a prison cell and boarded up the door
As we fight the same few inches of this broken neck of land.
A sergeant grabs him by the arm and pulls him to the rear
Where the weeping and sobbing hang heavy on the ear.

A mug of tea so hot and sweet he feels like he's been kissed:
Walter glugs it gratefully and wipes his dripping lips.
And feels a kind of happiness that Death took aim, and missed;
That Life clung on to Walter with despairing fingertips
As all around the air brimmed with the sound of letting go
Of sobbing breaths expelled from lungs that softly whispered
'No…'

Walter's ears are ringing and his head hurts fit to burst
But he sits and falls asleep at once, surrounded by the din
Of screaming. Walter's heard some sounds. This one is the worst:
The sky's just a container to keep the screeching in.
And yet in all this bedlam Walter sleeps and in a dream
He's walking with his Nancy in the sunshine by a stream

And as they walk her face begins to bubble and to burn;
Her eyes sink further down into her gaping, grinning skull
And she screams 'Walter will they never ever learn!'
Walter wakes up weeping and his head is full
Of the things he's seen that no-one should ever see
And he lies down in the shadow of a bent and broken tree.

Three days pass. Time moves on. The sky is still and blue.
Walter's sent back to the lines that wait to go again,
Wait to charge the enemy, those other people who
Are just like Walter and his friends, rows of frightened men
Who just don't want to be here, who'd rather be asleep.
War's a matter of expense. Soldier boys are cheap.

Walter's drawing furiously. Inspiration comes
At moment after moment as the tension fills the air:
Here's a crowd of infantry following the drums
There's a general in a huge and comfortable chair.
At his back a skinny child with horror on her face
Wiping at her eyes with a scrap of filthy lace

Walter's comrades pass the drawings round and round again;
They recognise their faces and the way that corporal stands
With his back to several generals as he pisses down a drain
As they try in vain to make him jump to their command.
Walter's drawings say the things his comrades never could.
They're simple and they tell a truth that can be understood.

Lars is still in Walter's mind: that moment when they met
Across a noisy foxhole and their drawings filled the space
That language couldn't speak of and history would forget
Even though the truth was staring right into its face.
And Lars remembered Walter, and wanted them to meet
After the war was over, just walking down the street.

They'd talk about their drawings, sit and have a drink,
Compare techniques and make each other smile.
At the things that people say, the nonsense that they think.
Somehow simple drawing could heal and reconcile
People who aimed bullets at the men across the way
Who made themselves a target every bloodstained day.

The summer sun rose up from the horizon like a ball;
The men began to sweat with fear and heat
And in the tight tense silence you could hear somebody call
'Hey Tommy: do you have nice things to eat?'
There was silence, then young Arthur's voice began to speak
'It tastes like next week and smells like last week!'

Laughter sounds the same in different languages, I think;
And laughter rose into the air that day.
The soldiers shouted insults, wiped their faces, had a drink
And wished that laughs would wash the war away
And Walter wrapped a cartoon round a brick
And Lars tied a cartoon around a stick.

Both were flung into the air to fly across
The No-Laughs-Land of No-Man's-Land like birds.
The javelin-throw, the chuck or the full toss
Delivering the comic and absurd
Reflections on a world turned inside out
'That was a good one!' hear the fighters shout.

A bombardment of drawings flew through the sky,
A barrage of laughter hung there like smoke.
All of us would rather chuckle than die,
We'd all rather weep at the power of a joke
Than shed tears of horror at things we've seen
Or tears of regret at just what might have been.

Then Walter stood up, stretched out and waved.
His mates gasped; cold silence held the trembling day
In its grip. The settled order had misbehaved
And the universe couldn't think of anything to say.
An unspoken line had been cut by a hand
Waving in the air over disputed land.

There was a pause and then a hand waved back.
It was real life. It just felt like a cartoon.
This could have been the signal for the moment of attack
But the morning sang to a different tune
As first Walter, then Lars, climbed the parapet
And walked into a meeting that the world should not forget.

Two figures slopping through the dragging mud,
On a day that seemed to hold its breath
Neither moving faster than the other one could;
Across a landscape slabbed and paved with death
They drew a line from a trench to a trench
From blood to guts to a scream to a stench,

They met in the middle and smiled and spoke.
Two languages melted in the summer heat.
They laughed even though they didn't get the joke
Then one drew the head and one drew the feet
Of a stupid officer with snot on his face
Not fit to be a leader of the human race

And one drew the hair and one drew the teeth.
And one drew the ears and one drew the nose.
A big wart on top and a beard underneath
And ludicrous expensive officers' clothes
Splattered with the parts of enlisted chaps
That get through the khaki's gore-proof gaps.

Then a miracle happened in the baking sun
And, like birds that flock when bread gets thrown,
The soldiers gathered to check what they'd done
And you'd have to have a heart made of solid stone
Not to be moved by the laughter and tears
Not to join in all the echoing cheers.

The soldiers said 'Draw me!' 'Now draw my wife!'
Lars and Walter drew and carried on making
Cartoons that were outlines of ordinary life;
Lars was sweating. Walter's hands were shaking
And men who hadn't laughed for weeks and weeks
Felt tears of sudden laughter trickle down their cheeks.

No photos exist of these moments of bliss.
Few words, just a handful from short letters home.
Just rumours, and stories. Just history's kiss
Placed on a cheek. No leather-bound tome
To examine the morning The Cartoonist's Truce
Stuck a spoke in war's engine and made it come loose.

Suddenly, scarily, all the men froze
In mid-chuckle, mid-laugh. A drawing half-done
Was dropped from the fingers as cannon fire rose
From the edge of the trees, the mouth of the gun.
And everyone turned and ran back to their places
The smiles and the laughter erased from their faces.

And life seemed to go on the same as before
But no-one forgot the day war held its breath.
Men put down their guns and men started to draw
And laughed at those slanted portrayals of death
Made in the spaces between men and men
And looked at and laughed at again and again.

It would be good to report that this story lingered
Here; a memory of hands across a muddy space,
Hands that took history, made it inky-fingered
With memories of cartoons, a smile on a face
A moment to dwell on as the war dragged on
A moment that returned when you thought it had gone.

We all know history's not like that. History's a farce:
People coming in and out through windows and through doors,
Standing up with dignity and falling on their arse
Slipping like a drunkard on a highly polished floor.
Walter should have gone home and made his drawing his trade,
Made enough to own a gallery, his drawings displayed

Should have kept in touch with Lars, created work together,
Visited each other's houses, shared a foaming beer
Talked about the intricate creation of a feather
With a pencil stroke until the meaning of the feather's clear.
Ah, the feather: the white one drifting down like snow.
Both these boys drifted into war. Both boys weren't to know

That war, this war, would send them wailing to their deaths;
No heroics, just a morning exploding into fire
That burnt them, burned their futures. Ragged, sobbing breaths
And paper rising in the wind. Rising, rising higher
Then disappearing in the branches of the shattered trees:
Drawings made from laughter, scattered on the breeze.

Imagine this, a pit village, 1919,
A row of veterans standing in the cold.
Several young men missing on the village green.
Several young men who will not grow old.
A young girl tight with weeping stands to lay a rose
By the station where they gathered in their Sunday clothes

By the station where Walter and his pals all went to war;
And Walter had his pencil, had his paper, had the thought
This would be the canvas where he really learned to draw,
The girl lays a rose for all the talent war cuts short,
All the poets, all the painters, who never stood a chance.
All the musicians silent. All the boys who never danced.